IMAGES
of America

ARMENIANS OF WORCESTER

IMAGES
of America

ARMENIANS OF
WORCESTER

Pamela E. Apkarian-Russell

ARCADIA
PUBLISHING

Published by Arcadia Publishing
Charleston, South Carolina

Library of Congress Catalog Card Number: 00-104054

For all general information contact Arcadia Publishing at:
Telephone 843-853-2070
Fax 843-853-0044
E-mail sales@arcadiapublishing.com
For customer service and orders:
Toll-Free 1-888-313-2665

Visit us on the Internet at www.arcadiapublishing.com

This book is dedicated to my aunt, Bizer Simonian, who, when all others failed, was there with photographs and information, as well as encouragement. Bizer's phone campaigns to obtain information and photographs was monumental and, indeed, this book could not have been completed without her help. It is for the survivors of the Armenian Genocide and those who work tirelessly for its acknowledgement. It is for those Americans of Armenian descent who carry their ancient traditions and customs and will not forget or let others forget the 2 million Armenians that were ethnically cleansed. It is for those who have helped and nurtured the Armenian Diaspora, championing them, understanding them, and soothing the pain and anger that lingers because their genocide has been denied and covered up, thus psychologically affecting all future generations and condoning genocide of all other minorities.

CONTENTS

ACKNOWLEDGMENTS

The author wishes to thank the following: Eva Haroyan for her encouragement, photographs, and her sleuthing for information; the Armenian Church of Our Savior for the loan of photographs; Bizer Simonian for her wealth of knowledge and the loan of photographs; Will and Abby Csaplar for the loan of photographs and historical information on Worcester; Sahag Davigian and Reliable Market for the loan of photographs; Lenore Burgess for the loan of photographs; A.K. Melikian and Mary Melikian, photographers extraodinaire—without their photographic genius, there would not be much documentation from the 20th century; and Christopher James Russell for photographing posters and items in his collection.

INTRODUCTION

Who were these Armenians that came to Worcester? When did they arrive? What type of place did they come from and why did they leave it? Why were they called "the starving Armenians?" Why were the Near East Relief, the Christian Churches, the Red Cross, and Ambassador Morgenthau so upset about their plight? In order to understand the people who came and how they became part of a city, it is important to know some of the history of a people whose genocide is denied, even today, by many with special agendas, thus denying them justice.

Two waves of Armenian immigrants came to Worcester, one after the genocide in Sassoun ordered by the Sultan Abdul Hamid in 1894, and the second as a result of the genocide, perpetrated by the young Turks between 1914 and 1924. This is not the story of the 1.5 million Armenians who were put to the sword because of their religion, but rather the story of the survivors. Who they were, how they reacted, and what they became was because of those atrocities. To understand the enormity of the genocide is to isolate areas and villages by number. Kerope, or Korph, was an average-sized prosperous village with 741 Armenian inhabitants; only 56 survived the carnage, and that was only because a few had been inducted into the army and escaped.

Worcester was a mecca to Armenians who escaped with little more than their lives. There were mills, there was work, and there were other Armenians who were struggling to make sense of what had happened to them. They were grateful to a new country that had held out its hand to them, allowed them to live, and taught them what democracy and the pursuit of happiness could be. America and Worcester opened their doors, and the Armenians who had escaped the deportations and massacres came from Kharpet, Urfa, Kerope, Malatia, Chimizgazak, and many other places that had been traditional Armenia and had become part of Turkey. These displaced people often came with little more than the clothes on their backs, but they were determined to survive. Their industry, their sense of humor, and their desire to rebuild families was why many felt that Worcester was America. Most immigrants came to Worcester first. Many moved on and many stayed. Those who moved on never forgot Worcester, as that was where their Americanism had been conceived.

The first Armenian Apostolic Church in America and the first Armenian Protestant Church in America were both founded in Worcester, Massachusetts. The Armenian Diaspora in America began in Worcester. If at first they were a trifle dysfunctional, it can be understood. They had seen their families murdered before their eyes; they had been robbed, beaten, and raped. Worse still, they had lost children and family members and they did not know if they were alive, dead, or had been sold into slavery and harems. They regrouped, built lives for themselves, prospered, and became a distinct flavor in the American melting pot. These immigrants dreamed of justice, but almost a century later, the Armenian Genocide is still denied by the perpetrators. Only one country has acknowledged the Armenian Genocide. Despite all the evidence and documentation, all other countries use the word "alleged" when referring to the Armenian Genocide. Adolph Hitler, while signing the order to obliterate the Jews said, "Who then remembers the Armenians?" Who remembers the Greek, the Assyrian, and the Armenian Christians who were starved, deported, and murdered because of their faith? The people of Worcester have remembered and have reacted the same as all that come into contact with the diaspora have.

Author William Saroyan once wrote,

> I should like to see any power of the world destroy this race, this small tribe of unimportant people, whose wars have all been fought and lost, whose structures have crumbled, literature is unread, music is unheard, and prayers are no more answered. Go ahead, destroy Armenia. See if you can do it. Send them into the desert, without bread and water. Burn their homes and churches. Then see if they will not laugh, sing, and pray, again. For when two of them meet, anywhere in the world, see if they will not create a new Armenia.

There are still survivors of the genocide in Worcester. Their children, grandchildren, and great-grandchildren have built a community that has enriched the city that has allowed and encouraged them to resurrect their culture, art, theater, music, and culinary treats, which have become part of the culture of Worcester and America.

The early years were very difficult. The first wave came not knowing English, had very little money, and went to work in the factories. Working conditions were exceedingly poor, the hours were long, and the wages were meager. Still, they managed to send money home to their families, educate themselves, and save enough so that they might one day be able to go back home and prosper in a land that offered them no justice or freedom.

When the deportations of 1915 began and the men were all slaughtered, those who were in Worcester raised enough money to send a few to help rescue those they could, via the Red Cross and other charitable organizations. Some were able to find their families or a few members, but the major part of a small nation was murdered, while the civilized world looked on with horror, but did little or nothing. Those who came had precious little, but they were grateful that they had survived and were given a chance to live in a country where soldiers did not come and take what you had, murder your family, and steal your women. They worked, built churches, opened businesses, had children, learned English, and became citizens. Coming from a harsh land, they arrived to see electric lights, automobiles, trolley cars, movies, and all the wonders we today take for granted. Seeing what they came out of and what they cam into explains why they were so grateful and uncomplaining in their new homeland, regardless of what hardships they endured.

For those arriving between 1915 and 1924, life was difficult enough. But in 1929, the stock market crashed and the Great Depression began. They had barely begun to adjust to their new life with its modern technologies. World War II saw many of the first generation of this "forgotten" people fighting for the preservation of a country they knew had to win, as they had seen the alternative and could not fathom going back to the nightmare of intolerance that had never ceased to appear in Pan-Turkic lands. From the Armenian Genocide to the Jewish Holocaust, the plight of religious minorities in the two allied countries of Germany and Turkey was a reign of terror. Within these pages, you will see "the starving Armenians" hold on to life with tenacity, lift themselves out of the blood bath, and preserve their species.

Worcester is a city heavily peppered with factories. These factories not only provided work for the immigrants, but also gave them a chance to meet and interact with other refugees and American-born workers. Here, they had to prove themselves as hardworking, honest people, worthy of becoming a part of this great nation.

At the same time, these were the early days of the union, before laws went into effect to protect workers. Industrial accidents happened, and no recourse was available. Times were difficult in many ways. Learning English and coping with a whole new way of life not only bound them together as a community, but also forced them to become a part of the life of the city. Churches were founded, plays were put on, dance troupes were formed, and picnics with live music and dancing were held. A frugal people, they opened businesses and educated their children to become professionals. Because most children were born here, due to the low survival rate from the genocide, the immigrants quickly became Americanized. Traditions were all important, but being American was even more so. The younger, American-born generation helped the older generation to cope with learning those new ways. Adapting and incorporating the old with the new made it an easy transition for the second generation on. These were Americans with a "shish kabab and pilaf" flavor, part of Worcester, the "all-American city."

The Armenian picnics were a cultural and integrating influence on both the Armenians and the area. These picnics continue even today and are attended by many non-Armenians who come for the food and the music. This is the gathering of the clans and all who would join in on their days of celebration.

In this poster, entitled *They Shall Not Perish*, Lady Liberty, with her sword raised, uses the American flag to protect a young Armenian girl from rape and genocide. This poster was one of many that hung in churches and public places in Worcester around the time of the Armenian Genocide.

One

WHERE THEY CAME FROM AND WHY

The Armenian people have been subjugated since the time of the Romans. Because of their location and religion, they have been purged from their native lands, which were annexed by the Ottoman Empire, Persia (Iran), and Russia. During the years of the genocide, they were expelled from those regions that had once been Armenia. They came from mountain villages and great cities, fleeing to any country that would receive them. Some stayed in those countries, while others moved on to France, England, and America. In order to know who the Worcester Armenians are, one must know where they came from, what they looked like, and what happened to them.

As the genocide proceeded, this poster was used to raise money to rescue survivors. This map shows the areas where the Armenians and other Christian groups, such as the Assyrians, lived before they fled to America.

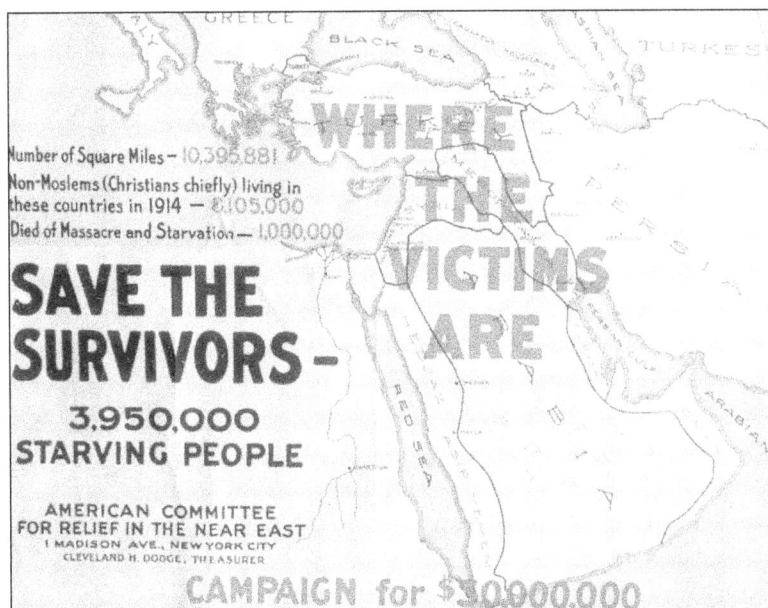

Number of Square Miles — 10,395,881

Non-Moslems (Christians chiefly) living in these countries in 1914 — 8,105,000

Died of Massacre and Starvation — 1,000,000

SAVE THE SURVIVORS —
3,950,000
STARVING PEOPLE

AMERICAN COMMITTEE
FOR RELIEF IN THE NEAR EAST
1 MADISON AVE., NEW YORK CITY
CLEVELAND H. DODGE, TREASURER

CAMPAIGN for $30,000,000

"The Child at Your Door"

400,000 ORPHANS STARVING
NO STATE AID AVAILABLE
CAMPAIGN for $30,000,000
AMERICAN COMMITTEE
RELIEF IN THE NEAR EAST

This poster, *The Child at Your Door*, raised funds for 400,000 starving orphans of the genocide.

W.B. King was the artist who designed this poster, entitled *Lest They Perish*. This Armenian woman with a child on her back prays while she walks past ruins of one of the towns from which she and many like her were deported.

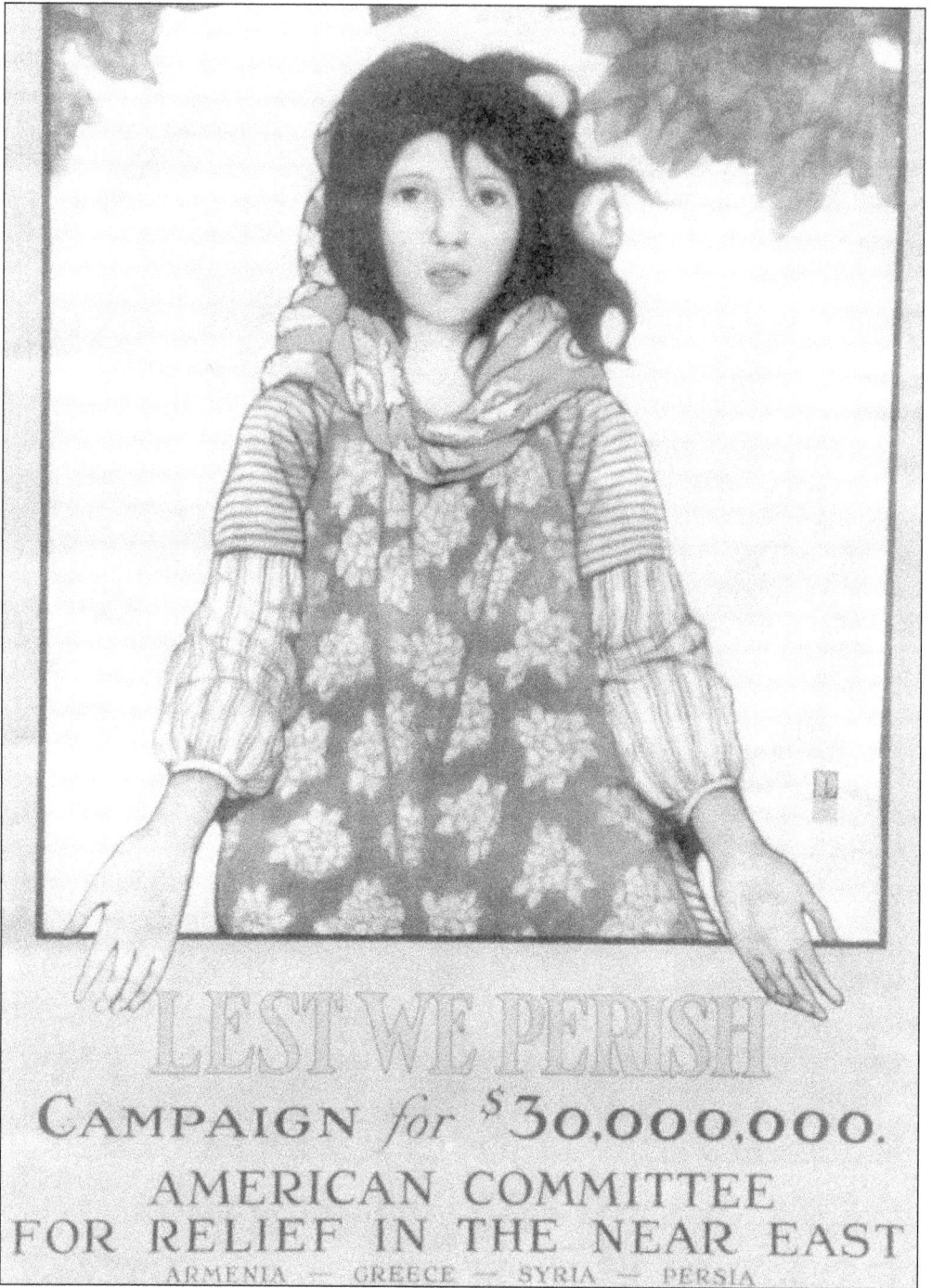

This Armenian refugee child stretches out her hands in supplication on a poster entitled *Lest We Perish*.

2 ½ Million Starving

Armenian-Syrian-Women-Children
17 cents a day will

Save a life !

Send contributions NOW to
Cleveland H. Dodge, Treasurer
American Committee for
Armenian and Syrian Relief
One Madison Avenue - New York

This poster for Armenian Relief was very common in its day. Since it is not as graphic as many others, very few have survived.

This studio portrait of an Armenian girl in Palestine is by Armenian photographer G. Krikorian, who was one of many Armenian photographers in the old city of Jerusalem.

دىوت مظدوى - حوي الشد

Harpoot Set No. 12 "Harpoot City from the West".

Both the city and province of Kharpet (Harpoot) were heavily populated with educated, affluent families. In this crossroads of the nation, many languages were spoken. Many missionaries made their homes in the area. Most of the missionary-funded colleges graced the area. Armenians, Greeks, Assyrians, Jews, and Kurds lived in relative harmony with each other under Turkish domination. Kharpet was a province and its major city was also called Kharpet, shown here from the west.

Unlike their Moslem counterparts, Christian Armenian women did not have to cover their faces and were less repressed. Many women were educated, which was very unusual for women in that part of the world. This image dates to *c.* 1907.

This poster shows David of Sassoun, a legendary mythical hero who slew his enemies and rescued the Armenians. Plaques, books, and pictures of this statue were displayed in Armenian homes.

Trebizonde was another area that was home to Armenians. This man and women are dressed in the clothing of their area. Very few of these costumes came to America, and the new immigrants began wearing American clothing right away. Armenian women re-created the costumes of the different regions for festivals and special events.

Brouusse's Armenian Quarter was fairly affluent, yet those who fled this area were lucky if they arrived in Worcester with $5 in their pockets. Often, the clothes they arrived in were given to them by the American Red Cross.

14. ADANA (Cilicie) – Quartier Arménien - L'Église Protestante.

The Armenian Protestant church, Adana (Cilicia), can be seen in the Armenian quarter. The missionaries were one of the main reasons many survived the genocide. Their protection and the funds they used to feed the starving made many converts. It was common practice for these brave missionaries to go out into the streets and bribe the army and the police to spare a person's life. The missionaries would harbor them in overcrowded churches or mission houses until they could bribe some other official to get them out of the country. The Armenian Diaspora owes these missionaries untold gratitude.

Noah's Ark landed on Mount Ararat, the symbol of the Armenian nation. When the Armenians first arrived in Worcester, they had pictures of the mountain printed as a symbol of their Christianity and freedom.

19

The twin peaks of Mount Ararat are symbolic of Armenia and its heart. It was here that Noah's Ark landed. Armenia became the first Christian country in A.D. 301.

Armenian Gen. Vartan Mamigonian defended the Armenian Church against its enemies. He died at the Battle of Avarayr. A copy of this famous picture is painted on the back of the stage at the Armenian Church of Our Savior on Salisbury Street. It serves to remind all who meet there for church social functions what Armenians have sacrificed for their faith.

Etchmiadzin is the mother church of all Armenians. In A.D. 301, Armenia became the first Christian nation. It is here that the Catholicos, the head of the Armenian Apostolic Church, resides.

Gomidas Vartabed, or Father Gomidas, has a special place in the hearts of Armenian churchgoers. He was the composer of one of the two musical services that are sung in the Armenian Apostolic church every week.

Gomidas Vartabed, seen here in typical clerics clothing, was a prolific composer of liturgical music and Armenian folk songs.

ՍՈՒՐԲՑ ՎԱՐՏԱՊԵՑ ⊚ KOMITAS WARTABET

ARMENIE

This image of a mother holding her child out of the water was often seen in the homes of both Armenians and those involved in the Near Eastern Relief. The artist Solomko rendered it to symbolize the suffering and losses of the Armenians.

Armenians, especially Armenian women, were often depicted in their ethnic costumes. As their non-Christian neighbors were not allowed to show their faces (because of their religious laws), Armenian women were easily recognizable. This image is an idealized Art Nouveau rendition.

Armenien

Ազատ Հայաստան - Armenia in Mourning

Mother Armenia (Myre Araxie) sits amid ruins with Mount Ararat in the background. This print graced many Armenian homes. It is called *Armenia in Mourning* and was from the painting made for the Armenian General Benevolent Union. This organization is still very active today, both in Worcester and worldwide.

That Belongs to Armenia!

In 1947, the World Armenian Congress produced this card. Pres. Woodrow Wilson points to traditional Armenian areas on the map that Turkey annexed—the region where most of the Worcester refugees came from. The term DP, or displaced person, was often used as a slur against the new immigrants, as many arrived with little more than the clothing on their backs. Ambassador Morgantheau was so upset with the cruelty of the Turkish triumvirate of Enver, Talat, and Mustapha that he quit his post and returned to Washington, where he worked ceaselessly to help the Armenians.

These Armenian women work a loom to produce a tapestry. Tapestries, rugs, lace, and other handmade items that the women produced found a ready market.

The Armenian alphabet was invented by St. Sahag and St. Mesrob in A.D. 405. This was 100 years after Armenia had become a Christian nation. Father Shumavian was the publisher of the first Armenian newspaper in 1794. The first Armenian book was pressed 500 years previously. One of the first things the Armenians did when arriving in Worcester was to publish their own newspapers.

This Armenian woman appears in traditional dress. Because of the mulberry trees growing in the areas they came from, silk was a major source of work. Her "Sunday best" dress would have been made of silk and han`dmade lace. Women brought this lace-making tradition with them, and that is one of the reasons so many pieces can be found, even today, in Worcester homes.

These Armenian men of Bortchald are dressed in traditional garb.

Bible-Women and Pupils, Garmooch

Perhaps these women never read anything except the bible before they arrived in America. When they arrived, however, they quickly began to read newspapers and magazines. Literacy was common among the Christian population, and the newcomers were eager to learn English. These women were from the town of Garmooch.

Эривань — Армянская семья за приготовленiемъ чучхело

Erivan — Famille arménienne préparant le tchoutchkhelo

At home, Armenian woman dressed in the regional dress of Erivan and in European garb.

This Armenian woman shows the gold coins that adorn her clothing and her fancy lace veil. When the deportations began, they were sudden. Many returned from church on Sunday morning to find their homes ravaged, and they were ordered out of town. What coins they had on them, if not stolen by the army or brigands, were those that adorned their clothes. These were all they had to live on and feed their children and elderly. The men were immediately taken away and slaughtered; the young boys were taken into the army and turned into Turks by converting them to the Moslem religion. Those who refused were slaughtered.

This Armenian woman came from Schemakhinsk.

These Armenian women, all of them barefooted, work at carding wool. This picture is one of the few the author has ever seen where people are smiling.

Three Armenian women appear in traditional dress. A person's style of dress revealed where that person came from. When Armenian women came to America, those distinctions disappeared, as they donned American styles and fashions. (It is unknown whether these three women were able to come to America during the genocide.)

SOLUCIÓN PAUTAUBERGE

This c. 1900 advertising trade card shows the Armenian Women of Erzerun at home. It was given as an inducement to purchase Pautauberge, a tuberculosis remedy of the day.

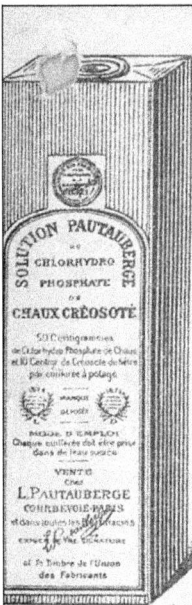

¿ QUÉ ES LO QUE NECESITAN
los DEBILITADOS, los FATIGADOS
aquellos que tienen débiles los
PULMONES y los BRONQUIOS ?
Un ANTISÉPTICO y un RECONSTITUYENTE
Para casos tales, nada como la

SOLUCIÓN PAUTAUBERGE

que en forma apropiada, reúne el antiséptico y el reconstituyente mas poderosos, la Creosota y el Clorhidrofosfato de Cal.

Constituye el remedio soberano contra los CATARROS, las BRONQUITIS CRÓNICAS, la GRIPE, el RAQUITISMO y la ESCRÓFULA. Aumenta el apetito y las fuerzas, agota las secreciones y previene la

TUBERCULOSIS

L. PAUTAUBERGE, 10, Rue de Constantinople, PARIS
y en todas las Farmacias.

Las Razas Humanas. — ASIA
Armenios de Erzerun

La raza armenia resulta del cruce de los semitas con los turcos, los turcomanos y los mongoles.

Viven en Turquía, en Persia, en Rusia, en el Sudeste de Europa y en ciertas partes de África. Tienen caracteres bastante típicos : estatura más que mediana, ojos y pelo muy obscuros, nariz recta o aguileña y boca ancha. Las mujeres, pequeñas en general, son muy guapas. El armenio tiene decidida vocación por la banca y el comercio.

Tuberculosis was a dreaded disease, and it was feared that some of the Armenian population might have it or be susceptible to it. Drinking this solution was to prevent and cure. Of course, claims like this could not be made today, nor could over-the-counter drugs like these be sold. There is no record whether this concoction worked, but in 1900 "cures" like this were common and could be found in all the stores.

5. serie de la "Turquie Libre"
Ecoliers Arméniens le 19. Juillet (v. s.) 1908.

In 1908, the Armenians supported the Young Turks in the overthrow of the sultan as they promised liberty for all. Not only did they deny them religious freedom, but only a few years later, they engineered the first genocide of the century, making the sultan's genocide of the Sassoun Armenians seem tame.

Bezalel Jerusalem Teppich=Atelier. Carpet weaving. בצלאל ירושלים

At the time of the genocide, the diaspora was still basically in the Middle East. There were many Armenians living in the Armenian quarter of the Old City of Jerusalem. Shown is a typical schoolroom of the time, where the children were taught reading, religion, and a trade.

31

This altar appears in St. James Church in Jerusalem. The Armenian Apostolic Church is one of the three custodians of the Holy Sepulcher. St. James is in the Armenian quarter of the Old City of Jerusalem.

R-1504-3005-The beautiful church of the Armenian Christians Jerusalem

Armenian orphans in Jerusalem serenade and thank American tourists for their humanitarian aid. The Near East Relief orphanage band can be seen at the railway station.

Грозното бѣгство на Турцитѣ при Черкезъ-Кьой.
En gare de Tcherkeskeuï: l'assaut d'un train à destination de Constantinople.
Flucht der Türken in Tcherkeskeuï

These Armenians are fleeing from their homes in the early days of the genocide, trying to catch a train to Constantinople. Many thought that by going to the capitol they could escape via ships, as there were large numbers of Europeans in the city.

In happier days, entire villages gathered together, sung, and danced in open or meeting area. Men gathered in one group and women in another.

The RMS *Pannonia* was one of the ships that brought refugees to this country. Noonia Simonian gave birth to a child on this ship; the captain named her after the ship. Pannonia was one of the first children born in the "new world." She was a British citizen because she was born on the high seas and had to wait until she was 21 years old to become an American citizen.

These Armenian orphans are aboard the USS *Olympia*. Many Christian denominations rescued children by purchasing them from their would-be murderers. They were then brought to other countries and brought up by the care and charity of that particular denomination. This explains why so many Armenians are members of denominations other than Apostolic.

The USS *Olympia* brought hundreds of orphans to America. These children were clothed and fed as a result of the unceasing zeal of the Near East Relief and other organizations.

Poor little hunger driven waifs appealing to the Near East Relief for bread.

Postcards such as this one were sent to people to ask for help saving these starving children. The term "starving Armenians" came about because so many starved to death in the deserts or on the death marches.

The Near East Relief bread line in Tiflis,   Transcaucasian, Russia.

Bread lines were lifelines for those who did finally escape the genocide. Most of the men had been taken out and killed; the survivors were mostly comprised of children, women, and a few elderly. This image was taken in Tiflis, Georgia, where many Armenians fled for refuge.

War Orphans at Derindje,   Turkey in the care of the Near East Relief.

The few boats available to evacuate the fleeing masses were used heavily. This raft held terror-laden children until they could be rescued. Taken in Derindje, these children were in the care of the Near East Relief Society.

These tables, end to end, would be over a mile long, of children fed by the Near East Relief.

Shown are children being fed by the Near East Relief. Many children who were not as fortunate as these perished of starvation.

CONSTANTINOPLE

TURKEY

Would you help a little boy?
One of the thousands saved by America through
the NEAR EAST RELIEF.

This child was one of many who survived because children in America donated their pennies and adults gave their dollars to save them from the scimitar. In classrooms and in Sunday school, children were asked to donate their pennies to help save "the starving Armenians." People raised these funds before there were organizations such as the United Nations, Unicef, or Save the Children.

To most Armenians, General Antranig was the greatest hero who ever lived. If it were not for his small, undertrained, undernourished, ill-armed army, many would not have survived. He came to America and lived in Massachusetts, then in California, where he died. His loss was felt greatly by the entire diaspora.

NEAR EAST RELIEF

1218 Little Building, 80 Boylston Street

BOSTON, MASS.

TELEPHONE HANCOCK 3280

INCORPORATED BY CONGRESS

THE LIGHT SHOULD SHINE BRIGHTEST AT CHRISTMAS

December 10, 1928.

My dear Mr. Stevens:

John Sharp Williams, Ex-United States Senator, said, "I think that God understands, and somehow finally forgives and loves all. But for that being so, I do not believe He could ever forgive European and American peoples for their conduct of base cowardice and betrayal ---- of their fellow Christians in the Armenian land."

But not all the American people were deaf to the despairing cry of the martyred Christians of Asia Minor. Some Americans organized the Near East Relief and sent the flower of their youth to the Bible Lands to feed the hungry, heal the sick, and raise a fearful and helpless remnant to hope and self-support.

Americans at home gave generously to hold up the hands of the workers in the field. Over a million lives were saved, over a hundred thousand orphaned children without homes or friends, preys to fear and disease, were taken into the hospitals and orphanages, were fed and trained, and are now the flower and hope of a regenerated land. Disease has been combated and in some localities stamped out; homes and farms restored.

Although the children still in our care range from seven to fifteen years of age (because it must not be forgotten that the sack of Smyrna was as late as 1922), we hope to outplace and provide for them in some way, so that this will be the last Christmas appeal we will make to you.

A Christmas gift to these Little Ones means life and hope to them; and uplift and joy to you. Perhaps you may give in the memory of some dear, Lost One.

Have the American people merited forgiveness? Surely not, if they grow weary in well doing, and at the eleventh hour fail to carry their magnificent undertaking to a triumphant end.

We need money. Please give all you can.

Sincerely,

Augustus P. Loring.

CHAIRMAN FOR MASSACHUSETTS

Please make checks payable to Near East Relief and mail in the enclosed envelope.

This 1928 letter from Massachusetts chairman Augustus Lorring tells why the Near East Fund needed money.

LETTER OF MISS FRANCES E. WILLARD.

Castile, N. Y., December 12th, 1896.

Dear Mothers and Sisters of America:

My heart is deeply stirred by the sacred ministry to the hapless little orphans of Armenia. Anything more piteous than their condition it would be impossible to conceive, and I pray with all my soul that our good and true people, White Ribboners and everybody else, may give their Christmas money not to fill the stocking of a child tenderly sheltered in a Christian home, but to put stockings on the bleeding little feet of pitiful Christian children who have no roof but the sky, no bed but the ground, and no food but the ground roots, except as we who are surrounded by every comfort reach out hands of help toward them and their heart-broken mothers. Let us ennoble and enlarge the hearts of our little ones by showing them how they can on this loved day carry out the Christ spirit. What we do must be done quickly. One dollar will feed, shelter and care for an orphan for a month. Twelve dollars for a whole year.

The above suggestion is equally appropriate for New Year's Gifts.

Send contributions for this object direct to BROWN BROS. & CO., 59 Wall Street, New York, marked: For the Orphan Fund of the National Armenian Relief Committee. For literature and further information write to Rev. F. D. Greene, Secretary, 118 Bible House, New York.

I sometimes fear least I plead too long, so I will make this short but none the less earnest, devoted and tender.

God bless you one and all and make your Christmas sweet in the happy homes that He has given you; and, better still, may it be hallowed by the knowledge down deep in your souls, that you have touched the keys of power that are vibrating in stricken Armenia, so that forsaken little children have food, clothing and shelter from the winter's cold. Let us remember the words of the Master, how He said: "Inasmuch as ye did it unto the least of these ye did it unto me."

Believe me ever with brightening hope,

Your Christian Sister,

FRANCES E. WILLARD.

This 1896 letter from Frances E. Willard explains that $1 would feed and clothe a child for a month. Willard, well known for her temperance work, was active, as was Clara Barton, in trying to save the Christian population of Turkey. There were 750,000 killed in this earlier, regionally segregated 1895 genocide; more than 1.5 million were killed in the second genocide, nearly one-half of the world population of Armenians.

Made in 1896, the front of this beaded
bag shows a brother and sister in
ethnic dress. Armenian handiwork
with this type of motif is very scarce,
as most purses were of flower designs.
The word *pahnt* means "prison," so it
is assumed that they were in a Turkish
prison, a prisoner of war camp, or a
refugee camp.

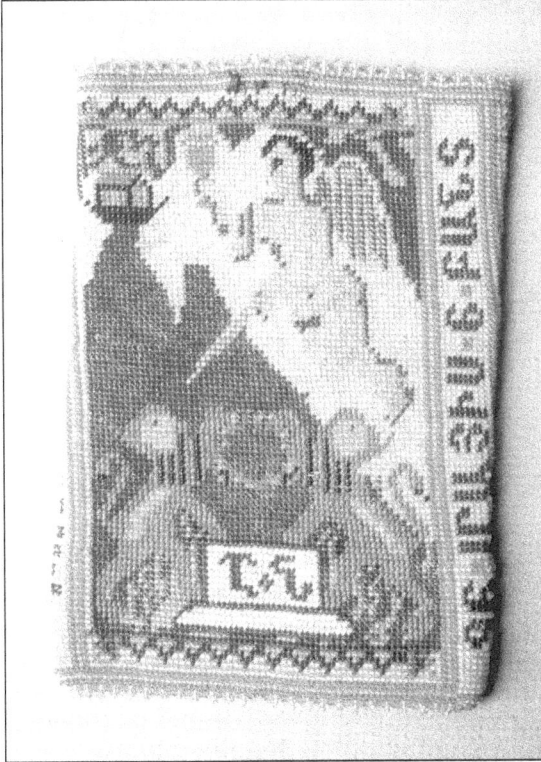

The reverse of the beaded bag depicts
Noah's Ark on top of Mount Ararat.
The angel with the chalice and the
sword represents the church. It is not
surprising that one of the leading
manufacturers of mesh purses was
opened not too far from Worcester by
an Armenian.

Armenian lace was famous from the Crusades on. Most of the women produced lace work for their homes and as gifts when they arrived in Worcester. The rare lace work is so much in demand that when items do come up at church bazaars, there is much competition for it.

Needlework was a common pastime for the early immigrants. Often, Armenian lace improvised on the traditional designs. This tablecloth was completed in 1947 by Noonoofar Simonian and was given to the author in the early 1970s. It is typical of this type of crochet work; embellishments were added depending on the skill and inclination of the creator.

This traditional altar was photographed in the Armenian Apostolic church in Batum, Georgia. The first church in Worcester continued on this tradition. The architecture of the Armenian church is very distinctive, and even the most modern renditions reflect that traditional quality.

M. Batoum. Armenian church. The altar.

This Armenian Protestant church was built in Ada-Bazar. The churches or denominations incorporated the traditional Armenian designs and were harmonious with the area they were in. There is strength and silent majesty in the designs that always keep them contemporary.

Église Arménienne protestante, Ada-Bazar

This print shows the Armenian kings. In the center is Etchmiadzin, which is the mother church. Above it is the Catholicos (Pope) of all Armenians, consecrating and anointing the king, who was the defender of the faith.

Тины Кавказа. Торня (пекарня): пурщикъ лелитъ лаваши, а другой достаетъ ихъ изъ...

In the old country, homes had *tohnehrs*, which were similar to a large hibachi set into the floor. Armenian woman continued to use wood-burning stoves to produce bread and baked goods (similar to those shown here) long after they arrived in America. They had gas and electric for the kitchen, as well as wood and coal stoves in the cellar for Saturday baking. In the old country, this was a familiar scene, as major baking was taken to places like this to be cooked. In America, the women set aside Saturday as baking day for the week and were delighted they could finish the entire process themselves. Bread was a staple. Small meat pizzas called *lahmehjun* and sweet buns called *chorag* were baked, wafting the wonderful smells to the entire neighborhood.

These dolls wear Armenian costumes of the Soviet domination period. Madame Alexander produced a doll for her ethnic series, but the costume is not very authentic.

Вид части города со стороны Ханскаго дворца.
Vue d'une partie de la ville prise du château du Khan.

Ахалцыхская армянка.
Arménienne d'Akalzik.

Баку. Bakou.

Типографія и Магазинъ Бр. Теръ-Ованесовыхъ, Баку.

An Armenian woman of Akalzik is shown in Bakou, now the capital of Azerbajan. At one time, the royal family of Armenia and Georgia were one and the same. Georgia is one of the few countries that has been tolerant and sympathetic to Christian Armenia and still has many Armenians living there.

Hotel d'Orient-Damas, Syrie

This postcard shows one of the many orphanages in which children worked for their living, producing oriental carpets, tapestries, and fabrics.

46

Two

THE ARMENIANS:
WHERE THEY WORKED,
LIVED, AND PLAYED

The first Armenians came to work, hoping to go back to the villages from which they came. Some liked it so much that they stayed. Later, with so many displaced Armenians, they flocked to Worcester, as this was America to them. From here, many moved on to other parts of the country, but none of them forgot the city they first came to and the miles they walked to work and play. The roots of Armenians in America began in Worcester and then spread out to the rest of the country. This is where it all began and where it continues to this day. Perhaps this is why so many Armenians come back to visit. The Armenians were dubbed the Yankees of the East by Rev. Albert Hitchcock on July 14, 1901. He thought of the Armenians as pilgrims looking for a new land for freedom and a new way of life. He could not have been more succinct.

In this World War I photograph of enlisted Worcester men, Nigholos Boghosian, Krikor Pilobosian, Sarkis Hayratunian, and Krikor Shaboian can be identified.

A Sunday school class at the Laurel Street Church poses in 1936. Pannonia Simonian was 15 when this picture was taken of her and classmates with their teachers and priest. Already, the

community had begun to grow with the birth of children and the adoption of orphans. Also, many family members were found by benevolent organizations and brought to America.

Nigholos Boghosian, seen in this WWI photograph, went to Fresno, California, and became a vineyard owner. He achieved the American dream and became a wealthy man. He was one of the first Armenians to achieve this goal.

Mr. A. Robert Apkarian, age 90, a genocide survivor, appears in front of an Armenian carpet. His one fond memory of his childhood was sitting on General Antranig's lap. He fled Turkey, got caught up in the Russian Revolution, escaped back into Turkey, and came to America with his grandmother and his cousin Roxy—all by the age of ten. He worked as a foreman on many large buildings in the Worcester area. He fled the cold Worcester winters to become a Floridian after he retired.

Those who were lucky enough to have been born in America felt at home with being both American and Armenian. At home, you spoke Armenian, and in public you spoke English. Being multilingual was expected. This studio photograph shows Oghda and Philip O'Gulian; Bizer, Eva, and Sam Simonian; and Carl Aiken.

Armenian silk manufacturer Bedros Manougian used this label on items exported to the United States. Worcester Armenian stores tried very hard to buy from those left in Turkey, as they knew how difficult things were for them. The American Orphanage helped support themselves by the sale of products such as these.

This 1930 photograph shows the Hunchagan delegation from Worcester at the Milford picnic. The organization came into being to protect, rescue, and help Armenians who fled the

Ottoman Empire. The organization continued to keep traditions alive and to insure the survival of the language, the religion, the culture, and the people.

Reliable Market on Chandler Street has been owned and operated by Sahag Donagian for 53 years. Previously, it was owned for 18 years by Baron Serop Boyajian, who sold it on April 20, 1947. At one time, the building had three floors above the market, with two apartments on each floor. These were all inhabited by Armenian families.

Sahag Davagian appears in his store, Reliable Market. The store has changed very little since the author was a child. The cheese, olives, *yalanchi*, and other Armenian foods are still as good as they ever were. Perhaps, the only change has been in the clientele, as more non-Armenians seem to stop for such delicacies as *bastoormah* and *toorshee*. At one time, the Chandler area was alive with small Armenian-owned businesses such as hairdressers, convenience stores, and shoe repair shops.

When the first Armenian church in America was built on Laurel Street, it was a cause for great joy and celebration. With approval from Etchmiadzin, the mother church, this church became the official seat of the diocese of America. The building was consecrated and the first mass celebrated in 1891. By the 1950s, the church became too small for the congregation and they built the current church on Salisbury Street.

The Laurel Street Church was built with a fundraiser, pledges, and a loan. It is now a Russian Orthodox Church.

The parish house beside the Laurel Street Church was where the priest resided and Sunday school classes were held.

The Armenian Church of our Savior on Salisbury Street was built in 1952 because the Laurel Street Church had become much too small for the growing congregation. It has expanded and now includes a parish house and a cultural center.

KhatchKars, stone crosses, dominated the landscape of the world's first official Christian country (A.D. 301). This *KhatchKar* was carved and dedicated in 1991 for the centennial of the first Armenian church in America. It faces Salisbury Street.

The Armenian Church of Our Savior Cultural Center was dedicated in 1968. It faces Worcester Polytechnic Institute on Boynton Street.

Norsigian Square is at the corner of Salisbury and Dean Streets; it was dedicated in 1950. The side entrance of the Church of Our Savior is shown.

Norsigian Square was named in honor of Pvt. George H. Norsigian. Norsigian enlisted in the U.S. Army during WWI. In 1918, at the age of 22, he was killed in action while fighting for his country. He was part of the 104th infantry.

The Armenian Church of the Martyrs Congregational Church at 22 Ormond Street (formerly Pink Street) was incorporated in 1892. It has continuously been a part of Armenian religious and cultural life in the Worcester area.

The Armenian Apostolic Holy Trinity Church at 635 Grove Street was dedicated in June 1979. The congregation had been located at 886 Main Street since 1948 in a building that had been the South Unitarian Church. The church is under the see of Cilicia and is home to the Armenian Revolutionary Federation. Holy Trinity regularly joins in with the other two churches for cultural gatherings.

Family portraits became very important to a people who had lost many loved ones in the old country and did not have photographs by which to remember them. Seen here are Yeghazar Simonian, his wife, Noonoofar, and their children, Pannonia, Ogdah, and Samuel. Yeghazar Simonian was delegated by his peers to aid the Red Cross with locating and bringing over survivors. He located his wife, Noonoofar, in Syria, where she had fled the death march through the deserts of Der Zor.

The Armenian Woman's Guild poses with Fr. Yeghishe Gizarian. Many of these women were genocide survivors. These were the women who, with their dinners, picnics, and social events, introduced Worcester to the joys of Armenian food. Organizations like this one worked long and hard after the Armenian earthquake to send clothing and medical supplies to the newly independent country. Their work has always bonded the diaspora worldwide. The organization was founded in 1908.

Robert Apkarian, president of the New England chapter of the Young Hunchag Organization, presents a trophy to Oghda O'Gulian of the Sparkey Junior League on August 23, 1938.

The Sparkey Junior League is shown at a picnic in 1938.

The flower girl in the front is the author at Ann and Sahag Sarkissian's 1951 wedding.

Ararat smoking tobacco was for those who liked to roll their own or could not afford the premade cigarettes. Men brought their smoking habit with them from Turkey. An Armenian made the blend for Camel cigarettes for R.J. Reynolds.

It is not surprising that this box of cigarettes, with the two peaks of Mount Ararat on the cover, has the brand name Ararat.

Worcester photographer K.S. Melikian took this group picture of the Social Democratic Hunchags (SDH) at their yearly gathering in 1930. The basic reason for the organizations was

to locate survivors and bring them together with family or to rescue them from deportation camps. Manoog Alexanian is one of the men holding the banner.

The Ashvantzees, or the people who came from the town of Ashodavan, pose in front of the Laurel Street Church, *c.* 1920.

The Armenian Maid.

Aurora Mardiganian

THE SOLE SURVIVOR OF THE MILLION ARMENIAN MAIDS WHO WERE TAKEN BY THE TURKS IN THE GREAT ARMENIAN MASSACRES

Shown are two pages from the sheet music for "Armenian Maid," published by the E.T. Paull Music Company. The music was part of the film *Auction of Souls*, based on the story of Aurora Mardiganian. This sad young woman often came to Worcester and was well known to residents.

Oriental delight or Loukhum is a sweet fruit jelly candy made sometimes with nuts and always with powdered sugar to keep it dry. Lemon, lime, and apricot flavors were preferred. Most often it was packaged and sold in small wooden boxes, but this was obviously a deluxe version to be packed in a fancy tin. The twin peaks of Ararat are again seen, as these mountains held a very special place in the Armenian heart.

Locumia Real Turkish Candy was sold in the stores in wooden boxes like this one. Very few have survived. The Armenian community quickly discovered American chocolate, and imports on items like this one decreased.

American companies like Ayers of Lowell, Massachusetts, geared their advertising toward ethnic markets, such as the Armenians. This *c*. 1900 trade card was for one of the many over-the-counter medicines that were popular and legal at the time.

ՏՕՔԹՕՐ ԱՅԷՐԻՆ ՍՌԹՍԱ ԻՆԱՑԸ

Աձը վէ եատոր նեպաթութան 'խպարէթ օլուպ հեր Նեվ սրթմայր քեսէր, ոոլուդ վէ սրձադ վէ ապըր վէ կլդի ՝ թմա վէ սրթմասան մէվլուտ 'կլէթէրի վէ դասատ պբրադապդպարը դնհրի աեֆ' եսեր։ Խ-թ'մայի ատա մուդիրը օ'մայուդ սրթմա քեսրէթի պաըունան մէմէ- քեթէրատ չ04 միսմա'ն՞ը ուր ։

Ս․ Մ․ Մխնատևան վէ չիսրեքեսսր Ամերիկան Մադադսսը Նօ․ 13 — եէնի ձամ՛ի՝ դաիուսր իթթխապ՛ն՞ատ ԴԱԼԱԹԱ, ԱՍԻԹԱՆԷ։

The famous Melikian studios photographed Rev. Agop Mekjian and his wife. They gave this card to parishioners over the Christmas season. Since the Armenian Church still uses the Gregorian calendar, Christmas is celebrated on January 6. Christmas carols are done in conjunction with the other Armenian Churches on the evening of December 24.

Vahe and Eddie Mekjian were the sons of Rev. Agop Mekjian. Vahe's dress was pinned, as he was old enough to start dressing in pants. This photograph was taken in 1924, just before they came to Worcester, where their father was to take over the pastorate of the Church of Our Savior.

Vahe, Eddie, and Alice Mekjian appear in this 1934 photograph.

This picture of Father Mekjian in his church robes was taken by K.S. Melikian Photographic Studios at 421 Main Street. A very modern and worldly man, he was able to move his congregation into a position of acceptability by those who still discriminated against the Armenians because of their names and their old-fashioned ways.

In 1944, K.S. Melikian Photographic Studios captured Vahe Mekjian in his American armed forces uniform. After the war, he became a barber in Worcester. One of the places he was located was at the old Union Station.

K.S. Melikian photographed Vahe and Mary Mekjian on their wedding day. They were married by the groom's father, Rev. Agop Mekjian.

Eddie Mekka appeared in the title role in *The Lieutenant*, a rock opera that played at the Lyceum Theater in New York City. Eddie won a Tony award for this part. He is probably remembered by most for his role on the television sitcom *Laverne and Shirley*. He played the part of Carmine and often had the opportunity to sing on the show.

Eddie Mekka appears below on the set of *Laverne and Shirley* in March 1978. In this episode, he played the part of a priest, in a way, following in the steps of his grandfather. He is with his mother Mary Mekjian, his sister Lenore Burgess, and her daughter.

The Mekjian family members shown in this c. 1949 photograph are, from left to right, as follows: (sitting) Kay with Dawn and Mary with Lenore; (standing) Eddie, Mr. and Mrs. Kosabian, Father Mekjian, and Vahe. The Armenian picnics have always been a gathering of the clans and a time to take pictures for those who had cameras. This was a period when the Armenian community was just becoming affluent enough to start having their own cameras. Few photographs remain from this period.

Music was a very important part of picnics and gatherings. *Harpoot to Istanbul* was the brainchild of Eddie Mekjian. He and his band played locally for Greek, Armenian, Jewish, and Asyrian functions.

The reverse side of the *Harpoot to Istanbul* album appears here. The songs may have been old, but they had been updated and the words spiced up. Mekjian's band was one of many that played at Worcester functions.

Mr. John Sisoian made this tinsel picture in 1940. He produced and sold these in the Worcester area. Unfortunately, they were seldom signed. This one was a wedding present and is identified on the reverse. His work was popular and graced many Armenian homes.

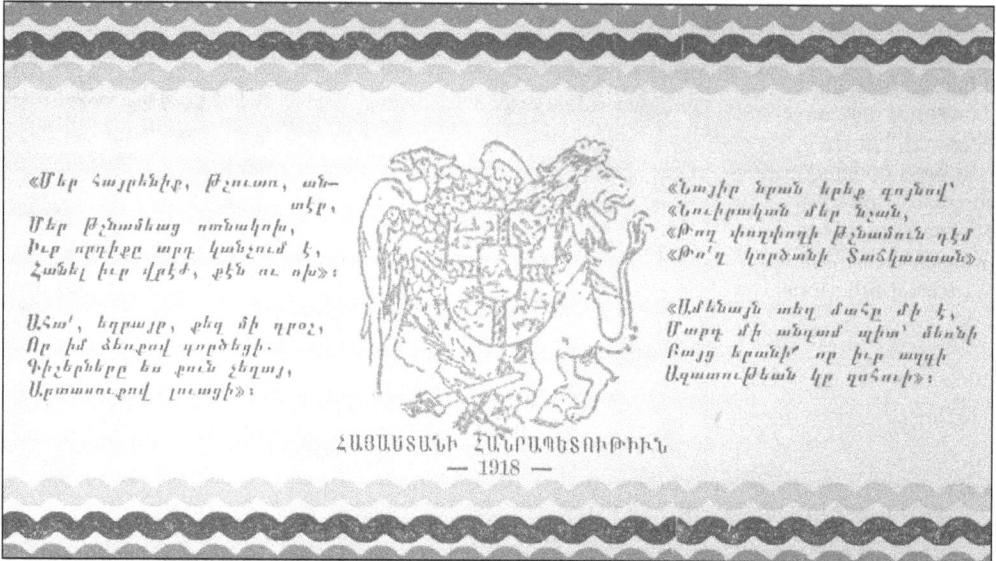

«Մեր Հայրենիք, Թշուառ, ան-
                              տէր,
Մեր Թշնամեաց ոտնակոխ,
Իւր որդիքը արդ կանչում է,
Հանել իւր վրէժ, քէն ու ոխ»:

«Ահա՛, եղբայր, քեզ մի դրօշ,
Որ իմ ձեռքով գործեցի.
Գիշերները ես քուն չեղայ,
Արտասուքով լուացի»:

ՀԱՅԱՍՏԱՆԻ ՀԱՆՐԱՊԵՏՈՒԹԻՒՆ
— 1918 —

«Նայիր նրան երեք գոյնով'
Նուիրական մեր նշան,
«Թող փողփողի թշնամու դէմ
«Թո՛ղ կործանի Տաճկաստան»

«Ամենայն տեղ մահը մի է,
Մարդ մի անգամ պիտ' մեռնի,
Բայց երանի՜ որ իւր ազգի
Ազատութեան կը զոհուի»:

The Armenian National Anthem was written by M. Nalbadian *c.* 1918. It consists of only four stanzas (1, 3, 4, and 7) of Nalbadian original long poem *The Italian Girl's Song.* It was written for a girl whose brother had gone off to the Italian war.

Mr. and Mrs. Shapazian appear in this K.S. Melikian photograph. It can not be emphasized how important this photographer was not only to the Armenian community, but to the city at large. If they could afford it, most community members went to the studios to have their picture taken. Very few Armenians owned cameras of their own and, even if they did, they could not photograph as this artist did. His daughter, Mary, was his student and has kept the family tradition alive.

Johnny Shapazian appears in his military uniform. Before leaving to go to war, many of the soldiers had their photographs taken by K.S. Melikian. As their futures were so uncertain, they wanted their families to have something by which to remember them. One of the major regrets of those who survived the genocide was they did not have photographs of their loved ones. Most soldiers hoped that by leaving this small token, it would alleviate the apprehension. Johnny returned from the war and became a barber in the Worcester area.

Krikor Apkarian had been orphaned by the earlier genocide and was caught up in the second genocide. As a political activist, he was on the most wanted list; he was also one of the few to escape hanging by the Turks. He fled to America and joined those members of his family who remained alive. He died in an industrial explosion during WWII, while working for the war effort.

BALKAN ARMENIAN . . . SPECIAL HORS D'OEUVRES
for individual or group (for Four shown)
ENGUINAR (heart of artichoke); Stuffed vine leaves and mussels; IMAM BAYELDI (Eggplant);
FASSOULIA POULAKI (white bean salad); BALKAN cheese and Olives.

Armenian food meant stores that sold the items necessary for such delicious meals. Bulgar, grape leaves, olives, string cheese, eggplant, and apricots were usually only found in ethnic grocery stores, such as Sahags. It was quite a while before bulgar, yogurt (*madzoon*), pilaf, and kabab made their way into cookbooks and the American culinary dictionary.

George and Anna Krikorian appear in this photograph. George Krikorian was owner of Spencer Industries.

In the early years, most Armenians worked for the American Steel and Wire Company. Usually, they walked to work, saving what money they could to help locate and bring over relatives, to establish churches, and to support social and cultural organizations. Very few were able to escape from Turkey with any valuables, so frugality was a necessity, rather than a chosen way of life.

Worcester, Mass.
Worcester City Hospital.

King, Queen, Pleasant, and Chandler Streets were the areas in which many of the Armenians purchased homes or rented. These streets are in close proximity to City Hospital, where they went in time of distress or need.

Many Armenian children were born in City Hospital, seen here with its surrounding areas.

City Hospital, with its wide, surrounding streets, was well traveled by those who would walk to the downtown area, to work, or to the Armenian American Cultural Club (AACC).

Bizer and Eva Simonian lived in one of the apartments over Reliable Market on Chandler Street until they moved to King Street. Their childhood recollections were of how happy they were. Few complained because they knew how poor their families had been during the genocide and that they were rich by comparison. "We never knew we were poor, as so many others were just like us" is what one hears from the genocide survivors and their progeny.

Sam Simonian appears with his four sisters, Bizer, Pannonia, Oghda, and Eva. Philip O'Gulian, in uniform, stands behind them. Sam was an air force gunner with a bomber crew in WWII when he was shot down and put in a prisoner of war camp. He was still in the camp hospitals when the invasion came; he had been abandoned there, still in traction, when he was liberated by the Allies from the bombed-out hospital. He was one of the many heroes to survive the war and never spoke of the horrors of the Germany camps. He was a plumber in the Worcester area and worked for many years at Camp Devens. He retired to Florida and is active in local politics.

Annie Krikorian, Rose Pilgian, and Eunice Hovanesian graduated from the Chandler Street School in 1938.

Mr. and Mrs. Davagian appear in this c. 1920 image. Hagop Haritunian has a child on his lap.

Gregory and Margaret Krikorian appear on their wedding day with Rose and Sarkis Aslanian.

Mr. and Mrs. Sarkis Bedrosian appear below with their son, Roosevelt, and Ohan Bedrosian, c. 1956. An educated, refined woman, she came to America and spent her life working on her husband's farm. Opportunities for Armenian women were very limited until WWII.

This group photograph shows the survivors from the Kharpet (Harpoot) area and their children, most of whom are first generation Americans. The photograph was taken by the

famous Worcester photographer, K.S. Melikian, in 1931.

The wedding reception of A. Robert and Pannonia Apkarian took place in 1940. The couple went on their honeymoon to the New York World's Fair with $15, of which $10 was borrowed! They recently celebrated their 60th wedding anniversary.

A wedding was an important event for many of the genocide survivors. Pannonia Simonian, although born on the high seas, was considered the firstborn of the "new" generation. Weddings like this one of Mr. and Mrs. A. Robert Apkarian in 1940 founded the hope for the survival of a nation that no longer existed. It was hoped that the next generation would insure that the "forgotten people" would survive and one day be acknowledged.

Yeghazar Simonian poses with his granddaughter in front of 35 King Street, just a few blocks away from the Oread City Hospital and Chandler Street. Many homes in this area were Armenian owned. Yeghazar lost his eyesight in an industrial accident.

Yeghazar Simonian and his three cousins—Sarkis, Garabed, and Katchadoor Yeghiaian—all came to Worcester in 1912. Yeghazart stayed in Worcester; Garabed went to France and died young; Khatchadoor died of poisoning; and Sarkis joined the Russians to fight the Turks in 1915 and was presumed dead. With the breakup of the Soviet Union, his cousin's family discovered that Sarkis left progeny.

In the year 2000 at the Armenian picnic at Institute Park, the faces have changed and the clothing is different, but the tradition of picnics and dancing is still very much a part of the culture. The nice thing about this type of dance is that everyone can join in regardless of age or gender. Those who do not join in the dance watch and cheer on the dancers. Traditional steps and words to the old songs may be forgotten and bands are not what they were years ago, but the communal warmth of such gatherings is still strong. It is a time and place for families to meet, reminisce about old times, and introduce their non-Armenian friends to their food, music, and traditions.

The 2000 Armenian picnic at Institute Park took place across the street from the Church of Our Savior. Shish kabab, losh, kabab, and khemah were some of the foods, made from recipes brought here from the "old country" and still relished today. In this photograph, Eva and Nona Haroyan enjoy the cuisine.

Art exhibits were common in the 1960s; this one was held in the park behind city hall. The author looks back with nostalgia to when this painting *The Maid of Cadiz* was exhibited there. The painting was purchased and its whereabouts is unknown.

Plays and amateur productions have always been popular. *Journey to Kharpet* was produced by church members for the amusement of friends and relatives.

Saroyanesque slapstick comedy has always been popular with the Armenian community.

Uncomplicated sets did not detract from Hye humor. Armenians are referred to as Hyes or Hyegagan after King Haig.

Three

WORCESTER:
THE CITY WITH WHICH THE ARMENIANS
GREW AND CHANGED

Technology changed the face of the city, and what was new and exciting luxury became an everyday acceptable necessity. The people who came in the 1880s and 1890s saw changes that those who came during and after the genocide did not. These changes included telephones, electricity, urban sprawl, the passing of the trolleys, and the changing of businesses on the Main Street. As the city changed, people's lives adapted to it. Each generation sees something new, and the old becomes obsolete. Today, Main Street is nothing like the author remembers it when she was a child. The downtown, which was such an exciting vibrant place, seems but a ghost of itself. Horses are no longer seen on the streets, nor are long-skirted Armenian ladies with kerchiefs on their heads. Times change, cities change, and immigrants become Americans.

For those single men who first arrived and could not find lodgings in boardinghouses, the YMCA proved a safe and comfortable place to stay until they could find other accommodations. This was also a place that many of the men came to socialize. The YMCA building appears in this 1910 photograph.

Centrally located, and close to the factories, many began the Americanizing process with the YWCA. When they first arrived, they were very badly discriminated against and called "dumb foreigners." Many Americans thought they were Turks and would act in an abominable manner. With so few of them here, the early days must have been sad and frightening for them. They had to prove themselves to be worthy of being allowed to become part of the city. This picture of the YWCA building on Chatham Street was taken in 1911.

Institute Park, across from the Church of Our Savior Apostolic Church was often the spot for picnics after church. Many a wedding picture was taken here.

92

Lake Quinsigamond was a popular area for spending a pleasant Sunday away from the toil of the factories; it was only a trolley or bus ride away.

Main Street appears in this 1916 photograph as some of the newly arrived refuges would have seen it for the first time.

This bird's-eye view shows an early-20th-century Worcester. For many, this world was different from the one they had known, and this difference in values and quality of life was a welcome surprise. Light bulbs, automobiles, telephones, and trolleys were but a few of the innovations that delighted the newcomer. It was a while before some of them were able to afford these luxuries. Walking and speaking to someone in person was still less expensive than the bus or telephone.

Elm Park, the first official park in the United States, was one of the many places that Armenian families enjoyed roaming through and enjoying their free time. Walking and picnicking were very popular with the Armenian community. In the 1920s, the women's guilds would meet in the park on nice days and often ran races. On the Feast of the Saints, they would come to the park, read each other's fortunes, and sing. Shown is the park in the 1940s.

Green Hill Park. General View, Worcester, Mass.

Green Hill Park in the late 1930s beckoned many Armenians as a lovely place to roam, talk, picnic, and visit with friends. Affluence was catching up with the hardworking Armenians, but the lure of parks and walks with the family was deeply ingrained. After church, it was quite common to go to an organized outing at one of the parks. The larger gatherings were at the Kaprelian Farm and then later at Maynard, where the author remembers the music and food with great nostalgia, as it was the highlight of her childhood summers.

University Park near Clark University was a pleasant walk. Many of the children went wading or swimming in the pond.

The Denholm and McKay Company, a Boston store, was not only a place to shop, but it gave employment to many first-generation American-Armenian women. Denholm and McKay sent this card in 1916 to their customers, informing them that their annual department managers sale would be from June 7 to June 10 and would be advertised in the evening papers of June 6, with seven full pages of the wonderful items available. However, circulars would be sent to those requesting them. One can imagine the amazement felt by the newly arrived immigrant at the splendor and grandeur of what was offered.

In 1912, most of the Armenians living in Worcester were men and the thrill of riding trolleys and attractions like the New Park Theater were of great interest to their families still living in Turkey. To those from farms and rural areas, Main Street was like walking into the future. Those returning to their native villages had great problems explaining such items as the electric light. One of the tricks they played on the new arrival was to ask them to blow out the light. When they could not do it, abetted by a co-conspirator, they would then seem to blow out the bulb. Naturally, it was switched off, leaving the unsuspecting victim quite perplexed. In 1887, there were 250 Armenians living in Worcester; all were men. The first two Armenian women allowed legally to come to America by the Turks were not until ten years later in 1897.

In 1918, the post office was a source of great civic pride and interest. Buildings like this one amazed the newly arrived refuges. In a few short years, they were not only posting cards and letters from here, but some of them would be working here. This image is rendered on leather and went through the mail on November 16, 1906.

Post Office, Worcester, Mass.

Walking was a way of life for the Armenians, and they often patronized this store, called Worth Cushion Sole Shoes.

The Worcester Theater, seen here *c.* 1905, changed little over the years, except for the posters and marquis. This theater was a very popular attraction offering vaudeville, plays, silent movies, talkies, concerts, and all types of cultural events. The newsreels were very popular with the Armenian community, as they were always newspaper happy.

Mechanics Hall in Worcester was a historic venue for some of the greatest performers of the day. Diversified in its entertainment, it not only provided cultural integration into the society, but was and still is a mecca for artists from around the world who enjoy the superior acoustics.

EMPLOYEES NOON-DAY LAWN PARTY
FACTORY of ROYAL WORCESTER CORSET CO
WORCESTER MASS

Armenian women worked in the factories to help support themselves and their families. During the Great Depression, these were prized positions.

When State Mutual Life Assurance on Main Street finally opened its doors to hiring Armenians, they were pleased to find that they were just another hardworking ethnic group in the American melting pot.

99

Because the Oread has burned down, many of the Armenians that later lived near its ruins never saw it as it is shown here. There was a playground with swings just below the ruins, and the women brought their small children to play there while they chatted and did their needlework. They referred to it as "the Castle."

Worcester, Mass., Holy Cross College, Fitton Field Grand Stand and M. J. Whittall Mfg. Plant.

Holy Cross College is located near the M.J. Whittall manufacturing plant.

The Worcester Market, c. 1924, was where major shopping took place. Corner stores, sometimes owned and run by Armenians, supplemented purchases from the Worcester Market. These small stores supplied the ethnic foods like bulgar, olives, lokhum, and other foods that were part of the traditional diet. The building has changed hands many times over the years, but the original ornamentation still appears on the building, keeping much of its architectural integrity.

This early trade card shows the incredible array of goods that were available from large department stores like Barnard and Sumner & Company on Main Street. They sold everything from dry goods to carpets or millinery items.

The Hurricane of 1938 did incredible damage. Buildings like the Unitarian church were in ruins, as were the homes of many Worcester residents.

Most of the first-generation Armenian children graduated from Classical and English High Schools.

Classical High School was severely damaged after the Hurricane of 1938. Children of all backgrounds were deprived of an education until other accommodations could be made for them.

Kane's furniture store and surrounding area were very badly damaged by the hurricane. Those working in damaged places were temporarily out of work while construction workers found themselves in great demand. Armenians who had been through earthquakes in the old country took this in stride and joined the community in helping recover from the devastation.

F. W. WOOLWORTH STORE

Front Street,   Worcester, Mass.

Many first-generation Armenian girls got their first jobs in the F.W. Woolworth store on Front Street.

The author remembers Main Street in Worcester from her childhood as it appears here. Main Street was an exciting place in 1960, with many small shops as well as the large ones like Filenes, Barnards, and Denholms. The Loew's Poli theater was the great attraction along this segment of the street.

The J.J. Newberry store can be seen in downtown Worcester in the late 1950s. Many Armenian women found employment in this store.

The J.J. Newberry Company at 10–20 Front Street was a five-and-dime store that many of the Armenian women frequented as they maintained a large selection of threads, crochet hooks, and other handiwork instruments that were so important to decorating their homes and making and embellishing their clothing.

The author remembers being taken to the Derby Grill at 19 Pearl Street with her brother by her aunts as a very special treat.

In the 1950s, the T & T Sea Grill and Restaurant was not only a longstanding landmark, it was still a meeting and dinning place for Worcesterites. This postcard gives a five-digit telephone number. It also invites customers to tour their "stainless steel, all electric, Hotpoint, most modern kitchen." Surely, many women did check it out—not only for the newfangled equipment, but to check on the cleanliness.

Worcester in the 1890s was already beginning to embrace the Armenian as a social group. Some came and stayed, while others moved on or returned to their native villages. Those attending Protestant churches had more opportunity to socialize with non-Armenians and often married into their families. The old train station in Worcester, regardless of what faith they embraced, was the point of entry into their new world. They may have disembarked in Boston, Ellis Island, or Providence, but they had not arrived until they stepped off the train in Worcester.

Institute Park, more than any other place in Worcester, has played a great part in the history of the Armenians. Here, they socialized and worked for Washburn Moen, which later became the North Works of the American Steel and Wire Company. A large proportion of Armenian men worked there, while the Norton Company was basically Swedish and closed to the Armenians. Washburn Moen found the Armenians good workers and happily hired them.

Washburn Moen appears in the background of Institute Park. The company drew water from the park for its industrial usage. In 1879, the first Armenian in Worcester, Aaron Yenovkian, began work at Washburn Moen and wrote to all his friends to come to the area. Some of these men who arrived were skilled laborers, tinsmiths, and wire workers and their skills were needed. One man arrived so skilled in English that he was hired on as office staff. Skating and hockey have always been popular winter sports in the park.

Trees are laden with ice on the southwest corner of Institute Park in the winter. Walking to and from work on days like this could not have been fun, though beautiful to behold.

The industrial stacks of the factory appear behind Institute Park. The men would take their short lunch break outside under the trees.

L.A. Ely's luxurious home faces Institute Park, which begins by the boulder. This home was a far cry from the small apartments, boardinghouses, and other places the men lived in.

Many workers appear outside the factory in winter in this image of Institute Park. The horse was still a major means of transportation and was also used and owned by Washburn Moen.

This close-up shows Washburn Moen and Institute Park. The cold winter months were no picnic for man or beast. Men cut ice for usage in these pre-electric refrigeration days.

Shown is a portion of land as it looked before it was incorporated into Institute Park in 1906.

The tower at Institute Park looks lonely and forsaken in this view.

The McFarlane House was located on Salisbury Street.

In 1898, this old city hall was taken down. Tearing down perfectly good structures has destroyed many historic landmarks. Times really have not changed; at least they have not put a parking lot or a mall in its place.

This real photo postcard of the North Works of the American Steel and Wire Company was mailed in 1906.

This postcard showing the first site at which barbed wire was made, was printed by Henry Freeman & Company of Worcester.

This 1911 postcard shows how close the factory was to the water. It was built close to utilize the water and decrease transportation distance.

This 1914 postcard of the American Steel and Wire Company gives an idea of the size of this one plant.

The American Steel and Wire Company appears in this postcard, showing the amount of area the North Works used and some of the nearby homes.

The South Works of the American Steel Company did not employ as many Armenians as were employed at the North Works. The community therefore emphasized the significance of the north plant.

This postcard shows a bird's-eye view of the South Works of the American Steel and Wire Company. No other company employed so many Armenians or was so significant in drawing them to Worcester. Many left as soon as they could and opened small businesses.

Harrington and Richardson Company was known for making guns.

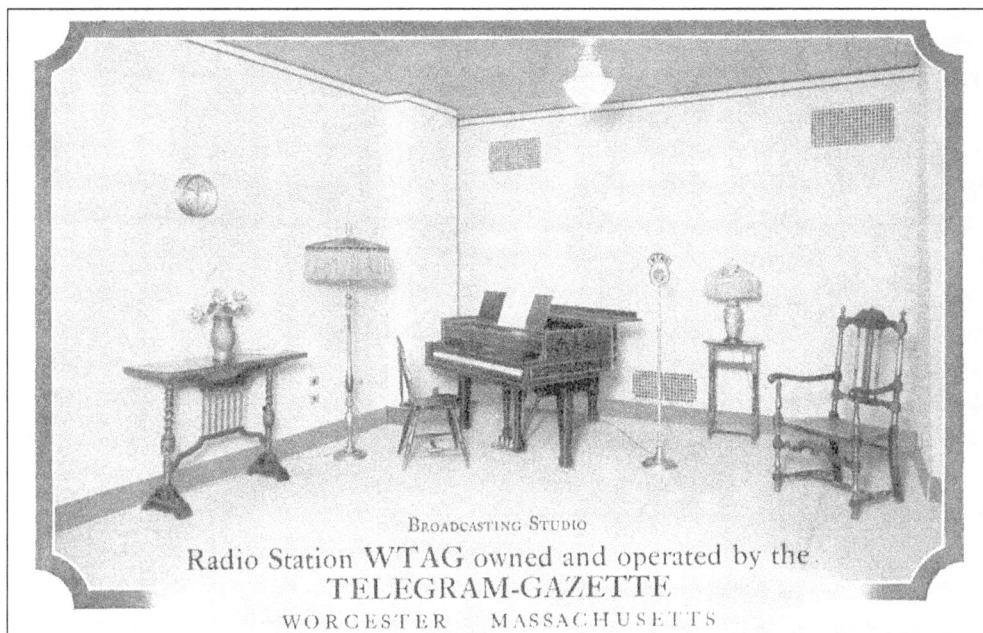

This postcard advertises WTAG radio and the Worcester Telegram and Gazette. Right from the beginning, this newspaper had covered Armenian events and reported on both the genocide and when there has been events honoring those who died. They have covered most of the important Armenian events for over 100 years.

The Old South Meetinghouse was located at the corner of Main and Wellington. Worcester was a very modern cosmopolitan city.

The Gardner Chandler House on Main Street was built in 1750. It was destroyed in the 1890s.

The Blackstone Canal closed in 1848 before any Armenians arrived, but many of them spoke of the Blackstone River that flowed through the city. Most people are not aware that the Blackstone River runs under the city of Worcester's downtown area. This copy was taken from a photograph of an original woodcut.

Park Avenue in winter looks completely different today, even when only compared to 50 years ago. This area is now built up with businesses, including an Armenian-owned Halloween outlet store.

One can imagine the amazement and interest that the new arrivals felt when they saw the modern advertisements and the quantity and type of items that filled the windows of shops, including the Latch Porter House in Worcester, shown above. It was impossible not to go window shopping for undreamt-of luxuries.

In 1906, the Granite Block on Main Street between Pearl and Elm Streets was taken down. Gaslights still lit the town and trolley lines added to the bustle of a busy city. A sign for White City can be seen on the side of the building, luring people to the very popular amusement park.

This orphans' home on Main Street was photographed in early spring.

The George Bancroft Rural
Cemetery is pictured here.

Davis Tower in Lincoln Park was
one of the many places that the
Armenians enjoyed walking to and
exploring. It was a lovely place to
read poetry.

121

Because transportation was so different and changed so rapidly in the 20th century, and because the Armenian men were so enthralled with the trolleys and trains, the author heard many stories of the wonder of them as a child. It seems only fitting that we view a few of these archaic eighth wonders of the world (as they were called) with such nostalgia by the author's grandfather and his peers. The men would come to watch the trains at the Consolidated Street Railway Carbarn.

This photograph shows the No. 220 City Line with two motormen standing beside it. One can understand the nostalgia they felt for these monstrosities. Most of us would love to enjoy at least one trip on it.

This 1912 postcard shows the students and motorman of the special trolley that went to Worcester Polytechnic Institute. The motorman was Lewis William Clark, father of David Myron Clark, who made the first pressure suits for pilots. The David Clark Company made the astronauts suits, and the author remembers her mother working there on them.

Two motormen sit in an empty car in this real photo postcard. The age of the automobile would swallow up the trolleys and make them a ghostly shade of the passing of an era. No wonder these men were so nostalgic for it, as it was the wave of the future when they arrived and soon was just a memory. Worcester changed and they changed. At least the horses were sent to the farms, not to the scrappers.

This Armenian actor plays the part of Hamlet. Presentations and plays were an important part of the cultural and intellectual life of Armenians. You have not lived unless you have read Shakespeare, Victor Hugo, or Robert Burns in Armenian.

SILGUIDJIAN, ISBENDJIAN & KEHIAYAN

FABRIQUE DE TAPIS D'ORIENT EN TOUS GENRES

Siège Social

SMYRNE

Succursales

CONSTANTINOPLE

SALONIQUE

CÈSARÈE

URGUB

SIVAS

STAMBOUL — TARAKDJILAR No. 76—78

Carpet and tapestry workers make their product. Those who lived in the capital Constantinople were slightly more fortunate than many others, as they were at a port and it was easier to escape from the country by ship. Being in Constantinople, it was more difficult for the genocide to rage full scale as many foreigners visited the large city. Many professionals, like these people, came to America and began their own businesses. This was an important manufacturer with offices in six cities.

Khrimian Harig is the affectionate name given to Father Khrimian. He was once invited to the home of the Pasha, who said if he made the sign of the cross over his food, he would be put to death. Father Khrimian smiled and said that the food looked so tempting, should he start here, or here, or here, or here, moving his hand forward, back, and side to side to form the cross. He did what he had to do, but they could not kill him for making the sign of the cross, as he had tricked them. He was a hero and a well-loved leader of the people.

This 1918 image shows, with symbolic surrealism, Armenia—what was happening to her lands and people at the time. The Red Cross nurse holding up the man was one the common images seen around the world.

This Armenian man wears a fez with Ararat on it. The fez was worn by all people in the Ottoman Empire. This fez may have been for a theatrical production or for the Shriners.

Krampus, or Grampus, must have been adopted from the Germans, as he accompanies Father Christmas and attends to naughty individuals. This image is quite rare. Perhaps there were not sufficient misbehaving Armenians to warrant his showing up more often.

FURTHER READING

Ararat Magazine, a quarterly cultural publication by the Armenian General Benevolent Union.

Avakian, Linda L. *Armenian Immigrants, Boston 1891–1901, New York 1880-1897*. A.G. Picton Press, 1996.

Charney, Israel. "Genocide Denial." (taped speech) David Barsamian/Alternative Radio aired on National Public Radio, April 5, 1999.

Deranian, Hagop Martin, Ph.D. *Worcester is America*. Bennate Publishing, 1998.

Gregorian, Arthur and Phebe. *Armenag's Story*. Lower Falls Publishing Co., 1989.

Hashian, Jack. *Mamigon*. Coward, McCain, & Geoghegan Publishing, 1982.

Morgenthau. *Ambassador Morgenthau's Story*. Doubleday, Page & Co., reprinted by New Age Publishing, 1919.

Ravished Armenia. Kingfield Press Inc. 1918. A movie of Aurora Mardiganian's life was made and is now lost. There is a substantial reward for a copy of it. The E.T. Paull Music Company
   song entitled "Armenian Maid" was written for this movie.

Saroyan, William. *Here Comes/There Goes You Know Who*. Trident Press, 1961.

Southwick, Albert B. *Once-Told Tales of Worcester County* Worcester. *Telegram and Gazette*, 1983.

Ternon, Yves and J.C. Kebabdjian *Armenie 1900*. Editions Astrid (French), 1979.

Thomajan, P.K. *Worcester Memories*. Cultural and Library Organization Armenian Church of Our Savior. 1983.

Werfel, Franz. *The Forty Days of Musa Dagh*. Viking Press, 1934.

EPILOGUE

In 1867, when the first Armenian arrived in Worcester, he was a curiosity. The early years saw men arriving in twos and threes to work at Washburn Moen Wireworks, which later became the American Steel and Wire Company. They suffered from homesickness and discrimination. When the genocide by the Young Turks began, large numbers came to join those who were already building a community. Today, the large Armenian population in Worcester descends from those who came to escape persecution and discrimination. They have built businesses, homes, and lives totally unlike those they would have been allowed had they not had the good fortune to come to America. They have become artists, writers, teachers, scientists, actors, doctors, housewives, plumbers, builders, and hairdressers. They have fought in wars and have served honorably in the armed forces. They have marched in parades and in honor of the "all-American city." They have become one with the city and the rest of the nation. Saroyan's words are true. The Turk was not able to wipe them from the face of the earth. Despite all that has been done to them, the pain and the suffering, the denial, they have arisen like the Phoenix out of the ashes and have been resurrected.